BEAR HUGS

FOR MY DAUGHTER

inspirio™

How could I say thank you enough for the gift of a wonderful daughter like you?

Every day I watch you grow is another

reason to smile.

I love you, daughter!

"As a mother comforts her child, so will I comfort you," says the LORD.

Isaiah 66:13

Love always protects, always trusts, always hopes, always perseveres. Love never fails.

1 Corinthians 13:7–8

We are heart to heart, hand in hand...

my daughter
and I.

We love because God
first loved us.

1 John 4:19

When God blessed
me with you, He blessed
me with sunshine.

I prayed for this child,
and the LORD has granted
me what I asked of him.

1 Samuel 1:27

Mother and daughter are two separate minds, unique and apart... yet joined at the heart.

Blessings crown
the head of
the righteous.

Proverbs 10:6

Thoughts of you
make my heart
overflow with
thankfulness and joy.

Mercy, peace and love be yours in abundance.

Jude 1:2

If I tell you that
I love you,
I wonder if
you know…
I mean it so
much more than
I can say?

There's a tenderness shared between mother and daughter that goes beyond words... and straight to the heart.

Since the day we heard about you, we have not stopped praying for you and asking God to fill you with the knowledge of his will through all spiritual wisdom and understanding. And we pray this in order that you may live a life worthy of the Lord and may please him in every way.

Colossians 1:9–10

Sweet moments
with you will always
be treasured.

Children bring their own love with them when they come.

Jean Ingelow

Like mother, like daughter
I've heard it said,
And if, my love, it's true…
I can think of no
greater compliment
Than to be compared with you!

I have loved you with
an everlasting love;
I have drawn you
with loving–kindness.

Jeremiah 31:3

My precious daughter,
I will hold you in my
heart forever.

The LORD your God is with you,
he is mighty to save.
He will take great delight in you,
he will quiet you with his love,
he will rejoice over you with singing.

Zephaniah 3:17

My daughter:
she takes the world
by storm—then
leaves behind a
beautiful rainbow!

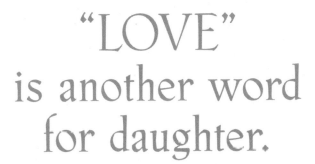

"LOVE"
is another word
for daughter.

Children are the hands
by which we take
hold of heaven.

How can we thank God enough for you?

1 Thessalonians 3:9

Your love
has given me
great joy.

Philemon 1:7

A daughter holds a
very special place
in my life...
in my heart...
and in my prayers.

I have no greater joy than to hear that my children are walking in the truth.

3 John 1:4

a daughter
is a gift
from heaven

Every child brought
into this world is a
new thought of God.

Kate Douglas Wiggin

I thank my God every time I remember you.

Philippians 1:3

If I could, I'd

write for you a rainbow
and splash it with all
the colors of God.

Ann Weems

You will be a crown of splendor in the LORD's hand, a royal diadem in the hand of your God.

Isaiah 62:3

My dear
daughter—
I love you
with all of
my heart.

Every child is God's miracle.

Philip Bailey

In a mother's heart God
plants his love;
in her arms he places a child...
then he watches as
**she grows
and grows
and grows.**

May the LORD bless you
and take care of you;
May the LORD be kind
and gracious to you;
May the LORD look on
you with favor and give
you peace.

Numbers 6:24–26 GNT

What feeling is so nice as a child's hand in yours?

Marjorie Holmes

SOURCES:

Bailey, Philip, *All Are Precious in His Sight*. Grand Rapids, MI, The Zondervan Corporation, 1999.

Exley, Helen, *A Special Collection in Praise of Mothers*, Selected for Hallmark by Helen Exley. New York, Exley Publications LLC, 1995.

Holmes, Majorie, *In Praise and Celebration of Daughters*, Selected for Hallmark by Helen Exley. New York, Exley Publications LLC, 1997.

Weems, Ann, *Reaching for Rainbows*. Louisville, KY, Westminster/John Knox Press, 1980.

Wiggin, Kate Douglas, *All Are Precious in His Sight*. Grand Rapids, MI, The Zondervan Corporation, 1999.